This workbook is taken from the class *Weekend Journey: Explore the Business Hero's Journey*. The entire class contains this workbook and a two hour audio. You may purchase the CD on Amazon.com or, you may upgrade to the entire class by visiting my website.

WEB ADDRESS:
http://businessstoryacademy.com/xtras/wj_ebhj_special/

Use the password "printspecial"

Contents

Introduction 1

Using the Business Hero's Journey as a Thermometer: 3

Where am I? 3

Using The Business Hero's Journey as a Compass: Where am I? (part two) 5

The Business Hero's Journey: Call To Adventure (Stage 1) 8

Using The Business Hero's Journey as a Map: How Will I Get there? 13

The Business Hero's Journey: The Road of Trials (Stage 2) 15

The Map: Using the Business Hero's Journey to Guide Your Way 23

    Forming Your Map 25

Business Hero's Journey: Triumph (Stage 3) 28

Business Hero's Journey: The Return Road (Stage 4) 33

Business Hero's Journey: Mastery and Freedom (Step 5) 38

Riding the Cycle: The Journey Repeats 43

The Business Hero's Journey and Your Business Wonk 45

Where do you go from here? 47

Begin your Better Business Journey 48

Note to the Reader

    This is a workbook. You are encouraged to write in this book. Highlight it. Make notes in the margins. Use it.

    Permission is granted to photocopy this book. Or better yet, use the information in the back of this book to get a PDF copy so you can print of the pages you want.

WEB ADDRESS:
        http://businessstoryacademy.com/xtras/wj_ebhj_special/

Use the password "printspecial"

Introduction

Welcome to your Weekend Journey: *Exploring The Business Hero's Journey.* This workbook is designed to help you discover the five main phases of the Business Hero's Journey. Additionally, you'll learn how the Business Hero's Journey can be both your compass (in terms of telling you your next step) as well as your thermometer (so you know how you feel). By the end of this workbook, you'll be able to identify the five main phases of the Business Hero's Journey, know which one you're in, and have actionable steps to move forward into the next phase.

What is the Business Hero's Journey?

The Business Hero's Journey is drawn from the Hero's Journey, a mythic structure described by Joseph Campbell's book, *The Hero With A Thousand Faces.* He researched the myths and legends of many people and found most of them have the same narrative structure. This same structure also can be found in many of our popular books and movies such as *Star Wars* or J.R.R. Tolkien's works. Though the Hero's Journey focuses on mythic or fictional stories, it also has strong applications in the "real world" too.

But we're not in the "real world" are we?

As spiritual entrepreneurs many of us deal with topics on a daily basis in which some individuals simply don't believe. There's an outside world, a muggle world to borrow a commonly used term, which believes we don't exist in the "real world". Topics like intuition, divination, and following your soul seem like "pie in the sky" concepts. And yet, we know they're not. We feel the power of our chosen tools and methodologies on a daily basis—often many times a day.

The Business Hero's Journey invites us to embrace the epic nature of the work we're doing. It provides a portal for us to create a fusion of the ordinary world in which we must do most of our lives and the magical one that we're creating through our roles as entrepreneurs. Within this portal we begin to work with our deeper, more spiritual nature as we evaluate where we've been and where we want to go.

In fact, the Business Hero's Journey also applies to our non-entrepreneur lives, which means that it becomes the tool through which we seek personal transformation, not just business growth.

That's what it is all about. Once we crossed the threshold and became entrepreneurs, we embarked on a journey that suddenly became not so much about business, but more about ourselves.

How to work through this Workbook?

The first time you sit down to go through this workbook, I advise going through it in order. Then, when you reach the end, we'll talk about how you can use this information to create daily practices and shifts. But moving through the workbook in order will bring you completely through all the stages of the Business Hero's Journey so you can better understand it.

Using the Business Hero's Journey as a Thermometer: Where am I?

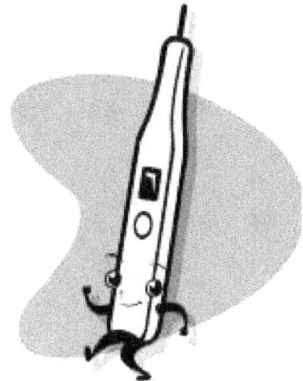

Before we talk about the actual journey you've undertaken, it's important to know where you are. Think of this section like the big maps in shopping malls with the red arrow pointing "you are here". In addition to knowing where you are, you need to know how you feel about it. As we'll discuss, some places in the Business Hero's Journey feel better than others. So knowing how you feel will help you find the steps to transition into the next phase of your journey.

So, let's ask the very important question.

Where are you right now with your business?

Your answer may be "just starting out" or perhaps it's more detailed, "I'm making great content, but I can't seem to get the word out.". I want to encourage you to be as detailed as possible. Detail will help you find focus and clarity on your journey. You'll more easily be able to see the next steps.

Where are you right now with your business? _____

_____

_____

_____

_____

How do you feel about this?

_____

_____

_____

_____

      This is the thermometer aspect of the Business Hero's Journey. It's important because once you name something, you are on the way toward knowing it. By naming your feelings and where you are at with your business, even if it isn't a happy place at the moment, you can ground yourself.

      It is important to remember that any time, but especially with this process, that you don't judge yourself for where you are at. Knowledge is an important part of our growth; once we're aware of something we can act. It's never "bad" or any other negative connotation to be where you are, even if you're dealing with a less than ideal situation. I encourage you to begin cultivating an awareness of this information in your business. Don't judge it. Simply let it be.

      Suggestion: *Take your business "temperature" regularly. Perhaps you do this at the start and the end of your week or at the completion of each project. The frequency doesn't matter so long as it's on a schedule that works for you. Then, use the map at the end of this workbook to plot your progress.*

Using The Business Hero's Journey as a Compass: Where am I? (part two)

In the sport of orienteering, where participants are given a map and a compass and told to navigate through a series of points (usually at speed), it's important to know where you are. It's even more important to know where you are headed because that's what controls the speed at which you can move.

It's not just orienteering that has this factor. Let's go back to that big map in the mall. You find the arrow that says "You are here" and then you look for the store's name that you want to visit. That's where you want to go, and with those two pieces of information you can plot the quickest route through the mall (or the route that avoids the food court).

You need to know where you are in relation to everything else so you can accurately plan your journey. There are times when it's good to simply be, to let your journey take you wherever it may. However, even then, if you're not sure where you're going, you could end up vastly off course.

Compass as True North

In a magnetic compass the needle always points north. By revealing where north is, the other directions become clear and you can move in your preferred direction. The knowledge of where north is isn't useless if you're not moving in that direction, because by simply knowing you can then make progress in your preferred direction. Otherwise, like the proverbial lost scout in the woods, you could walk in endless circles and wonder why you never get anywhere.

Your calling is your own true north. Sometimes we work alongside it, sometimes we move with it, but the calling itself is the north and around which we can orient the rest of our lives. The Business Hero's Journey is not a straight line to success. We've all seen those graphics showing points a and b with the squiggly, roundabout lines between them. Life isn't a straight line. But even when it seems like we've traveled this way before and are on the wrong path, we can use our inner north (our calling) to look at the Business Hero's Journey, and go "oh yeah, we need to go in this direction now."

What is your calling? Your true north?

_____

_____

_____

_____

Do you feel that you are on course?

_____

_____

_____

_____

How does your answer above relate to your "temperature"? In other words, how do you feel about your course and your place on it?

_____

_____

_____

_____

Your temperature and your compass work hand-in-hand to answer the "where am I?" question. The detail they provide will give you a firm grounding in the present moment. This opens the way for you to be mindful—remember don't judge—and make a decision on where you need to go from here.

Knowing where you are is a powerful wisdom. It means you are facing the future with your eyes wide open, shoulders square, and head up. You look forward—not to the past. And in doing so, you remain honest with yourself about your plans and processes. This allows you to plot your course along the Business Hero's Journey with joy, because you know where you are, which means you can see exactly where you're going. This is true even if you're not sure how your destination will look.

The Business Hero's Journey: Call To Adventure (Stage 1)

The first stage of the Business Hero's Journey is the call to adventure. However, it isn't just the call. There's a lot that can happen from the time we hear the call to share our gifts with the world and when we actually decide *and* begin to do it.

Though it may seem that this stage of the journey occurs only at the beginning, it actually happens throughout the entrepreneur's business career. Any time you launch a new class or product, there's a call to adventure. That's right—you go through the Business Hero's Journey every time you decide to change something in your business.

Don't let that fact scare you. Remembering the thermometer and the compass above, with those two tools, you can keep your journey going smoothly.

You can also be on multiple journeys at the same time. You have your business arc, that's the Business Hero's Journey you're on most often. But then you have smaller journeys with each product launch or change in strategy.

Stage One: The Call To Adventure

The actual call to adventure has three parts. First, you hear the call. But then you refuse the call. Yet the call keeps coming and so you heed it, crossing the threshold. This exhibits itself in the following process. Though this example is in teaching a class, you can substitute starting a business, or something else in your business for the class. The flow is the same.

I want to launch this really awesome class. (The call)
Who am I to teach this class? No one is going to come to this class. (Refusing the call.)
Of course I can teach this class. Let's go! (Crossing the threshold)

Or, you can think of this as three questions:

What am I called to do?
Why can't I do it?
Why am I going to do it anyway?

These questions create friction, a push-pull inside you as you go about the business of being an entrepreneur. Dealing with this push-pull is at the heart of your journey as a business owner. It's something every single entrepreneur needs to do. So let's look at these questions.

What are you being called to do? This question may not be as simple as it appears on its face. The answer to this question involves the gifts you are being asked to share as well as how you are being asked to share them.

What am I being called to do?

_____

_____

_____

_____

No doubt as soon as you received your calling, a thousand and one doubts emerged in your mind. It's easy to come up with reasons why we *can't* do something. Our minds excel at placing road blocks in our path.

The next step of the Hero's Journey is the refusal of the call. This is important; don't dismiss it. When we refuse the call, we perform valuable work when it comes to achieving our dreams. It's true. When the call is refused, we come up with all sorts of reasons why we can't do it. Then, if the call is strong enough and we follow our heart diligently, we will overcome all the objections our minds can give us.

Do not dismiss the refusal of the call. There are times when we're called and what we are being called to do really isn't part of our true calling. It's a "shiny" that distracts us from what we really want to do. This is much like the author who in the middle of writing a book gets an idea for a newer and better book, so she puts down her current manuscript to pursue the new one. In the middle of that book she gets another idea…and so on. You can see what happens.

How do you know if your refusal of the call is your denying your true gifts or something more productive, like staying on track?

Let's start with your objections and explore where they will lead you.

I am refusing the call because

_____

_____

_____

_____

If I do accept this call it will align me with my goals because

_____

_____

_____

_____

I can accept the call because

_____

_____

_____

_____

For each reason why you want to refuse the call go through and determine how the call will align you with your goals. Then, if it does align, think about why you can accept the call. How can you overcome your mind's objections?

Once you've done this for each of the objections (or reasons why you want to refuse the call), you will be ready for the third step, which is Crossing the Threshold. In this step you actually take the first steps toward achieving your goals.

__Suggestion:__ Remember that you "Hear the Call" and "Cross the Threshold" with everything you do in your business. Always take time to *stop, use the compass and the thermometer to make sure you know where you are on your journey and if you're still keeping the same heading.*

The next, and very important step is to actually *Cross the Threshold*. What does this mean? In simple terms it means you make the decision to actually embark on your journey. Often this is backed up with actions. If the call is for a new business, then domain name purchases, websites, even starting a blog all fall under "Crossing the Threshold" actions. For starting a new class or simply embarking on a new endeavor, then the "crossing" moment occurs when decisions are made and plans are put into place.

Let's look at your own "crossing" moments.

How am I deciding to "Cross the Threshold"?
_____
_____
_____
_____

What steps can I take to begin my journey as I "Cross the Threshold"?
_____
_____
_____
_____

Congratulations! You've completed the first stage of The Business Hero's Journey.

Using The Business Hero's Journey as a Map: How Will I Get there?

Before we move into the next parts of the Business Hero's Journey, let's pause and talk about the most important question we can ask.

How will I get there?

"There" refers to our destination goals, whether that's the successful launch of a new class or total financial freedom. It's one thing to say to visualize your future, to affirm and think happy thoughts about your eventual destination. Those tools help. However, many people become frustrated because they have no idea what that future looks like. Put too many restrictions on it and the universe won't have the freedom it needs to bring you the results you want. Too few restrictions, or not visualizing solidly enough and there won't be enough information for the Universe to work with. What's a business owner to do?

An Active Map

As we continue with this workbook through the remaining four sections, you'll find they form a map. However unlike a static paper road map which only tells you what roads there are and not, the Business Hero's Journey is more like an interactive map. It shows the roads, but it also shows dangers (or frustrating things like construction and toll roads). It's an active map, one which you can use on a daily basis.

I encourage you to experiment with the map. Focus not so much on the destination, but on the feelings. You may not know how freedom will look like for you. It's different for every person. But you do know the feelings of not having to worry about money or business matters. And if you really don't know exactly what it's like not to worry (Hey, I come from a serial-worrier family, too.), your focus can turn to peace or relaxation.

There is an emotion to find in each stage of the journey, and it's the emotion that you will either need to overcome, get through, or enjoy, depending on what stage of the journey you're in at the moment. This map may have stops on it. And yes, as an entrepreneur you'll find yourself in each of the stops at some time or another. But they're not vacation destinations like making sure you know what attractions you'll see and rides you'll ride at the local amusement park. They're emotions and you can visit them any time you want.

You will get there through daily practice.

Daily practice can be a dirty word to some people. Okay, two dirty words. However, it is also a vital piece of the puzzle in determining how we will get somewhere—what changes we will manifest in our lives, business or otherwise.

A Business Hero's Journey strives to answer the question "How will I get there?" When you don't know what the journey looks like it can be scary. Having no idea what to imagine when looking at various concepts can leave one to wonder if the visualization process will really work. Which is why a daily practice is vital. It will bring you closer to the business journey you desire, because every day you achieve greater clarity about your journey.

A daily practice can look like whatever you need it to. I recommend a few minutes of quiet centering, just listening. Asking "what do I need to do in my business?" will bring answers. Follow this by writing down those thoughts and your feelings about them. Feelings are very important as we'll see in the next stages of the Business Hero's Journey.

Joining a Business Hero's Journey daily practice in with a prosperity or abundance practice works well. The goal isn't to create yet another daily practice that you will have to follow. In truth, the actual goal is to create one encompassing practice that works for you, your mindset, and your business. There are no "wrong" answers when it comes to a daily practice that moves you forward.

Focus on the Feelings

The answer to the *how* question lies in the feelings you experience. Granted, some aspects of the Business Hero's Journey are more like a "dark night of the soul" or a shadow-journey where you must face your fears. These are not positive emotions to behold. However, these emotions do have to be faced. Acknowledging them—naming them—gives you strength. Denying them only makes them fester, ready to erupt at any time.

The answer to "how" we get to our business goal lives within the feelings. As you work through the rest of this workbook, honor where you are, no matter how bad it may seem. Give thanks for what you've come through and the breakthroughs you've received. And have hope for the future. For without hope, the journey is meaningless.

The Business Hero's Journey: The Road of Trials (Stage 2)

Many entrepreneurs live in the second stage of the Business Hero's Journey for a while. This stage is like when you make a resolution or start a program and a couple of weeks into it all of a sudden you hit a wall. Whatever you're doing becomes difficult. Frustrating even. It seems as if you aren't getting the results you wanted from doing the things you're supposed to be doing. This is also a stage of the Business Hero's Journey that many entrepreneurs fall back into even after breaking through. It's natural. And to get through this stage, we need to embrace it.

Let's face it. When we decided to heed the *Call to Action* and then *Refused the Call*, we knew we were setting ourselves up for a Herculean task. It's why we have the Business Hero's Journey—no simple ordinary journey will do for us. We're undertaking something that is done by a small amount of people. Most individuals don't become entrepreneurs, let alone spiritual entrepreneurs. By embracing our spirituality, honoring our gifts, and making the choice to share them with the world we already set ourselves up for something beyond an ordinary business venture.

Why then, do things sometimes seem so difficult?

Because spiritual entrepreneurs don't just want income; spiritual entrepreneurs seek transformation. And transformation always comes at a price. Gold must be melted down before it can be shaped into something new. Before you can make chocolate dipped pretzels, the chocolate squares need to be melted. Transformation happens.

Stage Two: The Road of Trials

I suppose we could trot out the old saying, "nothing in life is free" or a hundred other similar sayings. And there may be people reading this who think "told you so". There's also the belief that once you've "paid your dues" (whatever the hell that means in any given context) that you will no longer have to endure trials. At the risk of using a little profanity, I call bullshit on both of those beliefs.

Now is the time for honesty. When people say that entrepreneurship is the most powerful way to get to self-growth that there is, they're not kidding. Entrepreneurs who don't experience profound transformation and change no doubt did substantial work before becoming an entrepreneur. That, or they're living somewhere along Denial River, if you catch my drift.

In the epic fantasy movies *The Road of Trails* are all the obstacles that the hero (or heroine) needs to overcome before achieving the goal. For us children of the eighties, it's the training manage complete with a rock ballad. Think Rocky running up the Art Museum Steps. That's the *Road of Trials*. It doesn't have to be painful, though for many of us it can be. It does, however, require work—hard work—to get through. If we don't do the work before becoming an entrepreneur, guess what? We're doing the work now.

The Road of Trials Stage 1: Oh look, there's a road!

If you live in a rural part of the country, you may see those signs "county maintenance ends" or "pavement ends" and then the road turns into gravel. Even if it is a road maintained by the county, there may be obstacles. For example, I live 2 ½ miles down a gravel county road. When it's dry, you cross a bridge and about 1 ½ miles down the road there's a trickle of a creek right on a curve. In the winter, the creek freezes, and there's a moment of "whee!" as you go around the corner, even at a slow speed. The county also stops sanding the road in winter right at the creek. In heavy rains the bridge floods (It's a low water crossing.) and I'm so close to the state line that when I have to take the "back way out" along more county roads, I literally emerge onto the highway in the neighboring state. The moral of this story? Just because there's a road there doesn't mean that it's easily passible.

Such is the way of *The Road of Trials*. The emotion inherent within this stage of the Business Hero's Journey is frustration.

Why isn't this working for me?
This isn't getting any easier.
Why do these things always happen?

These are a few of the questions that may run through your mind as you embark upon this stage. The *Road of Trails* takes its strength from the saying, "what doesn't kill us makes us stronger." This is the strengthening part of the journey.

Let's take a moment to think about what trials you might be enduring in your business.

What isn't working for you right now?

_____

_____

What struggles are you facing in your business?

The goal of this step in the Business Hero's Journey is to persevere, to come out on the other side. When faced with a dark tunnel you have two choices: turn around and head back the way you came or to go through and emerge on the other side. On the Business Hero's Journey you need to go through.

What would be the biggest help to you right now?

How can you obtain it?

Don't be afraid to ask for help. There's nothing wrong with asking. In fact, there is more power in asking than in not. You'll get where you want to go faster and you will feel more supported.

When you don't ask for help is when you end up in the second stage of The Road of Trials. Let's stop that from happening if we can. On the next two pages pick your struggles and what you need help with. Write down what you need help with, what you will ask, who you will ask, and when you will ask. Refer to this sheet whenever you feel you are drifting down the *Road of Trials*.

There's a bonus worksheet in the PDF you can download by following the instructions on the last page of this book.

The Road of Trials Stage 2: Why am I inside this whale?

In spite of our best efforts, we can often end up in the second part of this sage: *The Belly of the Whale*. Much like the Biblical story of Jonah, in this stage we feel as if we've been swallowed by a huge beast and have no way out. Where the classic emotion of the previous stage is frustration, the emotion for this stage is overwhelm. We are drowning in things to do and places we want to go. It becomes too much, thus we feel as if we've been "swallowed".

Though I believe it's beneficial to take a look at how we got to this stage, dwelling on it will only increase our frustration and overwhelm. It is far more important to move forward. Once we're in a better place—further along the Business Hero's Journey—we can look back and see what happened.

The names we call this stage vary depending on our beliefs and the idioms we use. However, I feel *The Belly of the Whale* describes it perfectly. Think of a huge blue whale. Its ginormous compared to us. If it opened its mouth beneath a diver, it could very easily suck them in. Before the diver knew it, he or she would be inside the whale. A whale such as this is very emblematic of the way that situations creep up on us and then suck us in. Soon, we're in the middle of them—in the belly—and we have to figure our way out. Overwhelm works like that. We don't know we're overwhelmed until we are in most cases. Therefore, our focus should be on swimming out of the whale.

Overwhelm happens for a few different reasons.
- We simply have too much to do.
- We feel unsupported.
- We feel as if our efforts aren't moving us forward, that we're "treading water".
- We overcommit ourselves.
- We fail to balance work with personal time.

Overwhelm is not burn out. It can lead to burn out, but it isn't that emotion directly. When we are in *The Belly of the Whale* we ask, "How did I get here?". We don't say, "I can't go on." We are frantically looking for a way out of this stage, because just as we realize we've been sucked into the whale, we also realize that we're running out of metaphorical air.

The Belly of the Whale is an out stage. It's one that we need to get out of as fast as possible so we can find room to think and to breathe. With that said, it's time to look at the worksheet from *The Road of Trials*. Have you asked for help? Have you asked someone to help you get out of the whale?

What steps (one to three) can you take right now to get out of overwhelm?

_____

_____

_____

_____

Don't know what steps to take?

BREATHE

It may seem counterintuitive, but if you are overwhelmed stopping can help. When you stop, you can breathe. This creates space. In this space, you can then go back to what you wrote above and start taking one or two steps to get out of overwhelm. You can come up with a plan when you have time to breathe.

In fact, I'd encourage you to take "breathing breaks" throughout this entire stage of the Business Hero's Journey. They don't even have to be anything as defined as quiet, meditative places. Something so structured may actually work against the intent. Therefore, simply stopping and taking a deep breath. Then take another. Whatever it takes until you can have space to think again.

The Road of Trials Stage 3: "Don't wanna" syndrome

At some point during the *Road of Trials*, you encounter the last phase: *Temptation*. Whether you've just emerged from *The Belly of the Whale* and you think, "I don't want to do that again." or you are overwhelmed and frustrated and simply have a bad case of the "I don't wanna" syndrome, you get tempted.

Each person's temptation is different, but it also comes at a place where the previous two stages collide. The third stage of *The Road of Trials* is *Temptation*. This is the temptation to quit. Whether it's a week of "I don't want to do anything" or an "I don't want to do this anymore" thought, this stage is the temptation to quit.

Such temptation happens to everyone. Many times the decision to turn off the computer and do something else is a supportive one. Taking action, or a lack of action as the case may be, supports us in the long run. It's when we find it too easy to be in this stage of non-action that we succumb to the lure of temptation.

So how do you know if you're truly in stage 3 and facing the decision to quit or if you just need some time off?

You return to the compass and the thermometer. How do you feel? Where are you going?

Temptation: How do you feel?

Are you done with it just to be completely done with it or do you simply need a break? Do you still love the work you're doing? When faced with a case of the "don't wannas", taking your metaphorical temperature is the logical next step. This is done by examining how you are feeling about a given situation.

How do I feel?
Why?
How can I shift what I feel?

These questions will help you determine if you need a break or if you are in danger of walking away. If the answer to how you can shift what you feel is by stopping what you're doing, rather than "I just need a few days off", then you realize the temptation you're facing.

This is not an easy phase of the Business Hero's Journey. Often the pain of giving up is greater than the pain of pushing through the negative emotions, whatever they may be. In this case, a few days off may be exactly what you need. So long as the pain of giving up is worse, the next step is always forward.

There are no questions or workbook options for this phase. Simply ask yourself those three questions when faced with the temptation of giving up.

As we close out of this phase of the Business Hero's Journey, I ask you two questions.

Are you currently experiencing any phase of the Road of Trials?
_____

_____

_____

What can you do to shift yourself forward?
_____
_____
_____
_____

Congratulations! You are well on your way to being through the Road of Trials. The trials may come up again, but now, you are armed with the knowledge of what they are and can work to quickly shift yourself into a better phase.

The Map: Using the Business Hero's Journey to Guide Your Way

For many entrepreneurs, the *Road of Trials* is the most difficult stage. It comes early in the journey, at a time when most entrepreneurs doubt themselves and are still finding their way. This is why it can be one of the roughest stages. It's at this point when most entrepreneurs are just diving into their business and when they are at their most vulnerable.

Which is why it is so important to be able to immediately use the Business Hero's Journey as a map. Let's face it; no one wants to be on the *Road of Trials* for very long. Yet, when we're in this stage it feels like forever. It can seem like forever, especially if negative thoughts start to take over. That's why we need to find a way to use the Business Hero's Journey as a map—to stop those negative thoughts right in their tracks.

This brings us to the point of the Business Hero's Journey and that is to use it as a guide. Let's be honest. We're told as entrepreneurs that to get where we want to go we need to visualize it. However, we can't picture what we don't know. The Business Hero's Journey provides illumination as to what we can see in the distance.

In the front of this workbook look at the map of the Business Hero's Journey. Once you identify your place on the journey, you can then look at your next steps. Most people are looking forward to the end where mastery and freedom are found. It makes sense. We want to get to the good stuff.

That's okay, except a lot of times we're not in the good stuff. We're dealing with some aspect of the *Road of Trials*, or maybe further along the *Return Road*. The map helps us because we can look at the next phase, which will either show us the positive things that are coming or will alert us to something we may need to be on the lookout for. Then, we can plan a strategy for getting there.

The stage you want to attain and your strategy form the basis of answering the most important question: how. When it comes to visualization, making small, specific changes holds more power than thinking about something vague and fuzzy. Wanting something like a feeling of prosperity and imagining yourself in some future where you simply don't have to worry about money may feel good. There's also a really good chance it feels fake or far away. Instead of a general prosperity what is *one specific* thing you can do to move yourself toward that goal. Perhaps it is saving or budgeting for a dinner out. Maybe instead of packing your lunch, you stop by the local sub shop.

This is how the Business Hero's Journey becomes a map. With your thermometer and your compass, you will now move from stage-to-stage by looking at exact, incremental change. Big changes work too, but if you are having difficulties feeling that things are moving forward for you, then focus on the smaller changes.

Forming Your Map

A treasure map contains one really important piece of information—the X where you can find the loot. It may mark other things like islands or have a nifty dotted line for a path. But really, you're looking at a few pieces of information with an X for where you want to go. Your journey is kind of like that too. There's no way to predict what you'll find along the way. Your demons are not the same as someone else's. Therefore, your map will be unique, just like you.

Where do I want to go? What's my treasure?

_____

_____

_____

_____

Good. Now, we need to find out what you'll see on the way to your treasure. These are the sign posts. They may be emotions like joy and freedom. They may be physical things like a new car or that fancy new sign for your office. It may even be events, such as making a certain dollar figure.

What are the signs that I'm close to my treasure?

_____

_____

_____

_____

Every map has danger signs. Think about your own danger signs. What "evil monsters" would derail you from your journey? Again it could be events such as a loss of income or emotions like fear or worry.

My dragons are:

_____

_____

_____

_____

Put these together and you have a good picture of your treasure, the signs that you're getting close, and things to look out for. If you want, you can stop here. However, to get a real clear map, now you need to think about how you are going to get there.

What do I need to do before I can see the signs my treasure is near?

_____

_____

_____

_____

Now, you have a map. A road map to be precise. I would encourage you to draw it out. Paint it. Vision board it. Do something to make this map more than words on this paper. Make it real to you. Make sure that you can look at this map and really feel as if you will achieve your treasure.

Each point along your map will correspond with the Business Hero's Journey. As you'll see with the final three stages, once you past your *Road of Trials*, which is something every entrepreneur needs to go through, you will find each new stage to be one of learning and growth. Approach them with a sense of adventure. Look to your map as guidance.

Take the rest of this space to jot down some thoughts you may have about your map.

_____

Business Hero's Journey: Triumph (Stage 3)

Getting the checkered flag doesn't mean that everything is won. Sure, when the race is over *for that day*, the winner is the first one past the checkered flag. But the season continues and the race for year-end standings isn't won until the very last race. There are many checkered flags and finish lines before the final standings are out.

Such is the third stage of the Business Hero's Journey. Triumph isn't a complete and total triumph. There are still miles to go for that. It is a victory over the *Road of Trials*. As such, it should be treated like the win it is.

However triumph doesn't just happen. A series of events come together to create triumph. In business no one is waving a checkered flag or announcing that there's just "one more lap". We have to find our own finish lines, make our own progress points, and celebrate our own wins. It sounds exhausting, but it doesn't have to be.

Triumph Stage 1: Release the Brakes

The *Road of Trials* ends right before the release begins. Imagine if the car going around the track did so with one foot on the gas and one on the brake. It wouldn't be effective, would it?

Release is such a broad word. A lot of people, especially coaches, talk about release. When we release something, it isn't surrender. We are not giving up completely, letting someone else handle it all for us, or allowing someone or something to take over. Release is an active process where we shed something that isn't working for us. We remain in the driver's seat. The "something that isn't working" may be a need for control or a belief about our value. It could also be a process or program. For some, the release is a branding or even the way they're doing business. It doesn't have to be that drastic.

However, some release has to happen before the triumph occurs. It's a cycle. If we keep doing what we've always been doing, then nothing is going to change. So at its core, **release is giving up what isn't working for us with an active and conscious decision.**

Let's go back to the *Road of Trials* for a moment. At the end of the lesson you wrote down what your trials were and what steps you wanted to take to move forward, through and beyond those difficulties. No doubt there is some emotion that came along with those problems. Maybe it's overwhelm or frustration. Perhaps it's sadness or disappointment.

What would happen if you released that emotion? You completed the following section in the worksheet. I'm going to ask you to take that a step further.

What is your trial? _____

What do you need to release in order to move forward?
_____
_____
_____
_____

Keep this down to one word or less. Be as specific as possible. What do you really need to release?

If you're not sure, think about the one thing that if you could give it up would be like lifting a huge weight off your shoulders. It would be a breath of fresh air; you might even hear a choir of angels singing. There is most likely one thing that would do this for you. What is it?

Triumph Stage 2: Break through your barriers

When the weight is lifted from you, then you can make huge strides forward. This is the ideal time for a breakthrough. You're freed from the weight of the *Road of Trials* by releasing whatever has been holding you back. Newly lightened in spiritual and emotional load (and quite possibly physical) you have the space to breathe. It's in this breathing space that the breakthroughs happen.

You can't force breakthroughs. Too many entrepreneurs go searching for one, thinking that if they find "The Big Breakthrough" as advertised by coaches that they will own their power, make seven figures a year, and release whatever is holding them back. If it sounds too good to be true, it's because this kind of thinking generally isn't' realistic. The most powerful breakthroughs I've experienced have come in the quiet moments, when something is said, or a thought crosses my mind, that triggers an "aha moment". It's like a light bulb is turned on and all of a sudden I can see.

There is no fanfare that accompanies this moment. No trumpets. No choirs of angels. There is simply a dawning of awareness and something shifts in our lives. This is what a breakthrough looks like, and if you're looking for a ticker tape parade to occur when you have one…well, you need to create your own parade.

Your own breakthrough is waiting for you. Quietly, patiently it is waiting. You need to find it.

What did you release? _____

What changes are you seeing now?

_____

_____

_____

_____

Did you celebrate these changes? _____

The changes you're seeing are your breakthrough. Though I talk about "aha moments" and the light bulbs coming on, some breakthroughs don't even happen with that much notice. Sometimes we are working, going along in our lives, and realize that last week or last month something changed for us and we go back to see what happened. That, too, is a breakthrough.

Do not chastise yourself if your breakthrough was the quiet kind. Just because the immediate "aha moment" wasn't felt or sensed didn't mean that the breakthrough wasn't powerful for you. Celebrate any breakthrough—no matter how small. Sometimes the smallest ones turn out to yield the biggest benefits.

Triumph Stage 3: You did it!

The moment right after you realize you had a breakthrough is the moment of triumph. This may seem odd. There is most likely work that still needs to be done, even after a breakthrough happened. However if you think about the race analogy we used at the beginning of this section, even though the race was won the car still needs to be serviced, put away, taken home, and plans made for the next race. The car isn't just shoved into a trailer and that's it. *There is always movement and additional action to be done after a triumph occurs.*

So many entrepreneurs do not stop and celebrate the triumph. They are focused on the end goal, whether that's making enough money to leave a full-time job, getting X number of clients, or whatever large goal they have set for themselves. The large goal is nice. Really nice in most cases; however, it isn't the only goal in an entrepreneur's journey. It shouldn't be yours.

The key to this stage of the Business Hero's Journey is to recognize the triumph when it occurs. We talked about breakthroughs being soft and quiet or loud and big. Triumphs run the same way, too. All of a sudden you could be writing copy and you realize that your mindset shifted. That happened because of a breakthrough and *it is a triumph.*

Our goal in this stage of the Business Hero's Journey is to celebrate the triumphs. Up until now we've been dealing with some powerful, and sometimes difficult, concepts. The *Road of Trials* is never easy. Coming through release to get to a breakthrough isn't easy either. Breakthroughs can be rough; the Tower tarot card tells us this. Triumphs by their very nature are moments to savor.

Do you recognize your triumphs?

What recent breakthrough have you had?

_____

_____

_____

_____

What was your triumph?

_____

_____

_____

_____

How did you celebrate?

_____

_____

_____

_____

Do not put a limit on your triumph. It doesn't matter if you had a huge triumph, such as surpassing a big milestone on your newsletter or a small one. Celebrate it. In fact, as we move forward through the rest of the stages, you'll notice that my mantra to you becomes "Celebrate it!"

So, put down this workbook and celebrate all the triumphs you've had. And yes, getting this far in the workbook is a triumph in and of itself.

Triumph Stage 4: Bliss Baby, Bliss!

Are you savoring your triumphs? Or do you have a win and then rush onto the next goal? If it's the latter you're depriving yourself of valuable bliss. Yes, I said bliss.

Frankly, bliss is something that's missing from most entrepreneur's lives. Is it missing from yours?

Bliss is the final stage of triumph because it is what happens after the triumph. When there is a win, there should be a celebration. When the celebration is over with there remains a glow. This is the bliss. It's the moment when you have accomplished a major goal, acknowledged it, and now move forward enveloped in the joy this brings.

Too often, entrepreneurs skip bliss. It doesn't bring in money and it doesn't gather clients. They wonder why bother and move on to the next actionable, marketable goal. Bliss is the fusion that happens when business processes and spiritual processes work. Bliss is where the mojo starts to get going. If you don't get to bliss, it will be difficult, if not impossible, to finish the rest of the Business Hero's Journey.

My question to you?

How are you going to enjoy your bliss?

Business Hero's Journey: The Return Road (Stage 4)

Having attained *Bliss* (sometimes more than once), in dealing with pure interpretations of the Hero's Journey the hero faces an important question—does the hero return to bestow the knowledge and rewards that he gained upon his fellow mankind?

For the business hero, the question is similar.

Does the Business Hero bask in the bliss, or does s/he take the lessons learned forward in the business?

This may seem like an odd question. Of course the Business Hero would move forward. Right? Not necessarily. Too often, especially if the celebration or accomplishment is a large one, it is tempting to simply stay there. "I have my website and opt-in page up. I'm done," this entrepreneur may say. Yet, there is a way to go before we reach the final stage, and most likely a long way to go before the entrepreneur reaches her goals.

The Return Road is the decision the entrepreneur makes not to sit on her laurels, but to move forward with whatever it takes to grow her business.

The Return Road: The First Curve (Refusal To Go Back)

You've never driven on curves before until you've driven in the mountains. They don't have to be big mountains like the Rocky Mountains, but a smaller range, or an older one like the Ozarks or Appalachia would do, too. For a girl from a state composed mostly of flat farmland, coming down to the Ozarks was like all of a sudden riding a roller coaster every time you went into town. Take one of those curves going sixty and whee! Eventually you learn how fast you can take the curves and which ones really require you to obey the speed limit signs.

The first curve on the Return Road is like that. It's an acknowledgement that you are passing some sort of threshold—almost like when you heeded the call in the first stage of the journey. You are not going back to your old life. Ever.

And yet, beyond that curve, that new life you so want to live, is uncertain to you. It's a completely different process. Perhaps you're moving from being full-time employed to completely self-employed. Or maybe it requires a move across country. Whatever it requires, it's scary. And you're not quite sure you're ready.

Then there are those gifts, those lessons you learned in the *release* and the *breakthrough*. It'd be easy—too easy—to sit where you are and say "I did it", but you know there's more out there. And you are dying to share that more with others.

So you make the curve.

You refuse to go back.

You are determined.

You got this.

Do you really? Let's check.

What are you ready to leave behind from your old life?

_____

_____

_____

_____

What are you ready to embrace as part of your new life?

_____

_____

_____

_____

What gifts are you bringing with you to share?

_____

_____

_____

_____

How will this impact your business?

_____

_____

_____

_____

Okay, take a deep breath. You've made it around the corner. Except, this is all new and you're not sure what's going to happen. You've made it to the second curve of *The Return Road.*

The Return Road: The Second Curve (Reaching Out For Help)

You realize you need a guide or an ally on this road that you've plotted for yourself. You're so close to achieving your goals, and yet you feel so far away. The second curve in the return road happens when you realize you need help and yet you refuse. After all, we can come up with so many reasons why we don't really *need* help.

It's a luxury.
They're just false claims.
No one can really help me make that kind of money.
I know how to do it.
I can't afford it.
I'm not one of "those" people. I'm independent.
I don't know what kind of help I need.
Coaches are for people who don't know where they're going.
I have plans. I don't need help.

The reasons go on and on. I bet you have a few of your own. You may even believe them. There is also probably a part of you that recognizes standing at the start of a curve, wondering if you really want to go on and see what's around the bend. In fact, I'd be that you recognize your need for help.

One of the biggest skills to achieve before you can reach mastery (Which is part of the very next stage, so you really are *that* close to achieving it if you're here.) is learning when to ask for help. Actually, there's a good chance that asking for help when you need it is a positive skill for life.

It is important that at this stage on *The Return Road* that we release anything which might hold us back from freedom and mastery. A "go it alone" mentality is very much a part of that.

What do you need help on right now?

_____

_____

_____

_____

What is stopping you from asking for help?

_____

_____

_____

_____

I'd advise you to stop for a moment and simply think about this last question. There is something, perhaps many some things, stopping you from asking for help. There's no shame in that and nothing to feel badly about.

Perhaps this is the biggest hurdle outside the *Road of Trials* that entrepreneurs face—dealing with their own demons when it comes to asking for help. Even if they don't identify with being "Type A", asking for help is difficult. When asking for help, it can bring up many different issues such as…

Trust
Feeling silly
Feeling stupid

Worry

Fear

Acknowledge this when it happens. Give yourself space and care. Understand why it is happening. And work to release these emotions. Asking for help doesn't have to be scary. It doesn't have to make you worry about your business.

When you are able to ask for help, you can then move forward with support in your business.

Ways to ease the fear of asking

- ✓ Remember that everyone needs help sometimes. No one knows everything.
- ✓ Ask for referrals. Utilize your network.
- ✓ Make notes. Don't be afraid to follow your own advice.
- ✓ Know when to honor yourself and your boundaries. Some well-meaning help simply doesn't resonate with you or your business.
- ✓ Don't be afraid to experiment.
- ✓ It's not failure. It's a learning curve. You can, and will, go on.

When you have said no to your past life and sought out the allies that you need on this journey, then you are ready to move onto the next step of the Business Hero's Journey.

Business Hero's Journey: Mastery and Freedom (Step 5)

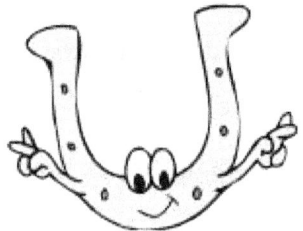

The final stage of the Business Hero's Journey comes in two parts: mastery and freedom. This is the moment that most entrepreneurs want. It is here that the final results of all the hard work comes and the rewards are beautiful. Some will call you lucky once you reach this stage. They may ask how you did it?

And to someone who is on a prior stage of the Business Hero's Journey it certainly does seem like magic to get to a place where there seems to be more pleasure than pain. Some roads, as you are well aware, are tougher than others. Which makes it important to acknowledge reaching this place on the journey and to demystify it for others who haven't quite made it here yet.

The truth is that there is no magic elixir, no magic program or success code which will catapult someone into this final stage of the journey. It comes through inner and outer work, both professionally and personally. Sometimes this stage happens quickly and you're there, reaping the rewards. Other times this stage seems to take forever to arrive, making it difficult to enjoy once it does.

Mastery and Freedom: I got this!

In the final stage of the Business Hero's Journey, the entrepreneur finally encounters the two things that she (or he) have been wanting for a long time: mastery and freedom. Mastery comes first. Mastery comes not in a diploma or in a book learning sense, but rather in the sense that "I got this" no matter what comes up in the business.

This doesn't mean you know everything. Who does? What mastery means in terms of the Business Hero's Journey is that you feel confident that you have the tools at your disposal to find out the answers and take care of most anything that comes up in your business. Even if you don't know the answers, you know where to find resources.

You are comfortable with the flow of your business and its direction. You feel like you're doing good work and can't wait to do more. That is what Mastery means.

There's a good chance that you're not there yet. That's okay. Very few people make it to Mastery without working at it and getting comfortable with their business. Even if someone achieves Mastery, there will be times when it feels elusive, as if it's slipped out of his or her grasp. That's why we talk about the Business Hero's Journey being a journey that repeats itself and we move in and out of various stages. More on that later.

Entrepreneurs often ask two main questions when it comes to *Mastery*.

How can I get there?

How can I stay there?

The roadmap/compass/thermometer system of the Business Hero's Journey answers those questions quite well. The first question relies on the road map system I've been talking about. The goal of *Mastery* isn't to actually know everything. No one can do that. The goal is the emotions of accomplishment and competence. You feel accomplished because you've gotten to a specific point in your business. You feel competent, because very little worries you in your business. Whatever happens you know you got it under control.

Therefore, to answer the first question, you must ask yourself about those two feelings.

What have you accomplished in your business?

_____

_____

_____

_____

What do you want to accomplish that you haven't yet?

_____

_____

_____

_____

The path to *Mastery* lies between those two questions. Just because you haven't accomplished the goals you want, doesn't mean you aren't going to. Finding the steps to bridge the gap can be an accomplishment (or many) in and of itself.

Take one thing that you want to accomplish. What are the steps you need to take to get there (or just get started)?

_____

_____

_____

_____

Good. We're not going to put too many things on the plate. Simply look at this one item and these steps. Do they seem achievable? Do they seem reasonable? Do they seem doable? Remember, asking for help is part of our previous stage, *The Return Road*, so this means you shouldn't be afraid to ask for help, not if you want to move forward into *Mastery*.

Suggestion: Don't get hung up on where you're not. Instead, focus and work on where you ARE and what skills you need to move into the next stage. Refer back to your steps. The gap between where you are and where you want to be is not a barren wasteland. It's a place full of opportunity and promise.

Based on what you wrote above, as far as where you want to be and the steps to get there, what does Mastery look like to you?

_____

_____

_____

_____

Now, do something really important. Take that picture of what Mastery should look like to you and disregard it. The "stuff" of the picture…let it go! The emotions are what you want to keep. It's the emotions that will hold you in good stead as you move forward. The "stuff" can change. Perhaps you find that instead of a house on the beach you find a cute home in an artsy community that suits you even better.

Mastery and Freedom: This is what I've been working for!

Much like *Mastery, Freedom* can sneak up on you until you realize that you are living the life you wanted. *Freedom* is the final emotion of the Business Hero's Journey and *Freedom* is all about the emotion. When you've achieved *Freedom* as an entrepreneur, you are in full control of your destiny. It doesn't man bad things won't happen. It means that you lack worry about money and you have enough financial resources to take care of whatever you need to. There's no stress over a home or car repair that comes up out of the blue.

Freedom is the stage that everyone wants to get to and many don't know how to achieve. It's also the scariest stage. What does *Freedom* look like? How would it feel? And honestly, what would you do if you don't have to worry about money or time anymore?

Those are weighty questions brought to you by this final stage of the Business Hero's Journey. For a lot of entrepreneurs, it's easy to dismiss them. After all, everyone wants to be free from money worries or pressures on his or her time. But when it comes to feeling those emotions, there's a good chance that fear arises.

The key to achieving the *Freedom* stage of the Business Hero's Journey is to create space to honor any emotions that come up, not to tag them as "positive" or "negative" and to be open to however this manifests for you. Let's look at how we can do that.

What does *Freedom* look like to you?

_____

_____

_____

_____

Take a few moments to contemplate the image you just created. Remember, don't judge or attach any positive or negative connections to it, or to where you are right now. Simply allow this image to unfold in your mind.

Can you think of one or two things you can do in order to be closer to your vision of *Freedom*?

_____

_____

_____

_____

    Now that you're starting to think about the things you can do in order to bring about this final stage. Think about what you can do on a daily basis to bring you closer to the image of *Freedom* you want to achieve.

    Freedom isn't a stopping point; it's a springboard designed to take you back through the Business Hero's Journey. Now that you're here, don't rest on your laurels. Keep moving. Keep seeking out new business challenges. Begin the journey anew with the next phase of your business.

Riding the Cycle: The Journey Repeats

The Business Hero's Journey is not a straight line. Yes, it is a journey from point A to point B with some stopping places in the middle. However, it isn't meant to be a one-way trip. Having just gone through the workbook, you may think that it'll be exhausting to be dealing with the Business Hero's Journey on a continuous basis. Keep in mind that you're already on this journey. You have the big journey of your business from launch to achieving your goals. With each new aspect, for example a new product or a new program, you go through the journey again.

The point is not to fear the cycle, but to embrace it. Become okay—not just okay but in love with—wherever you are at in the journey RIGHT NOW. To do so will open you up to finding the resources you need.

All stages of the Business Hero's Journey have positive aspects. Each of the stages has something to teach us. The trick is not to get hung up on how tough or difficult one of the stages is compared to the others. Yes, it is different, and no it isn't always easy. But even something as beautiful as *Mastery* or *Freedom* can be difficult. Each person will find the different stages to be unique, even if they've actively gone through the journey several times.

Some tips will help you navigate the repeating and concentric journeys.

1) Know if it is a big journey or a little one in scope, not in impact.

Even the smallest journeys can have a large impact. The scope will be different for a new product release in an already established business vs. setting up a complete business from scratch. If the journey is a large one, then be prepared for smaller sub-journeys to take place within it.

2) You can be in multiple places on the journey at the same time.

There is nothing that prevents you from facing *The Call To Action* when dealing with a new product or offering, *The Return Road* on your larger journey, and close to *Mastery* in getting your free opt-in gift up. You can be in multiple places at the same time.

3) Provide space to honor your feelings.

Whatever your feelings are—HONOR THEM. Don't judge. Don't wish you were elsewhere/felt elsewhere. Simply allow them to be. Sometimes you have to grieve for aspects of your business that you are giving up or that don't work for you, and you have to embrace what does working. You can do those things simultaneously. Wishing you were "happy" or "positive" all the time simply shuts down those other emotions so they can't get cleared out. Eventually that emotional closet will burst and you'll be forced to deal with them. This makes the journey more difficult, so deal with those emotions in the first place.

Suggestion: Take a blank piece of paper and draw a large circle on it. This is your largest business goal and the largest (and probably longest) Business Hero's Journey you are on at the moment. Then, within it, draw circles representing other journeys you may be on, such a product lunch or a new offering idea. You may end up with a larger circle containing smaller concentric circles with additional circles inside. Keep this image in mind so you don't become overwhelmed by the layers of the Business Hero's Journey.

A sample image is below.

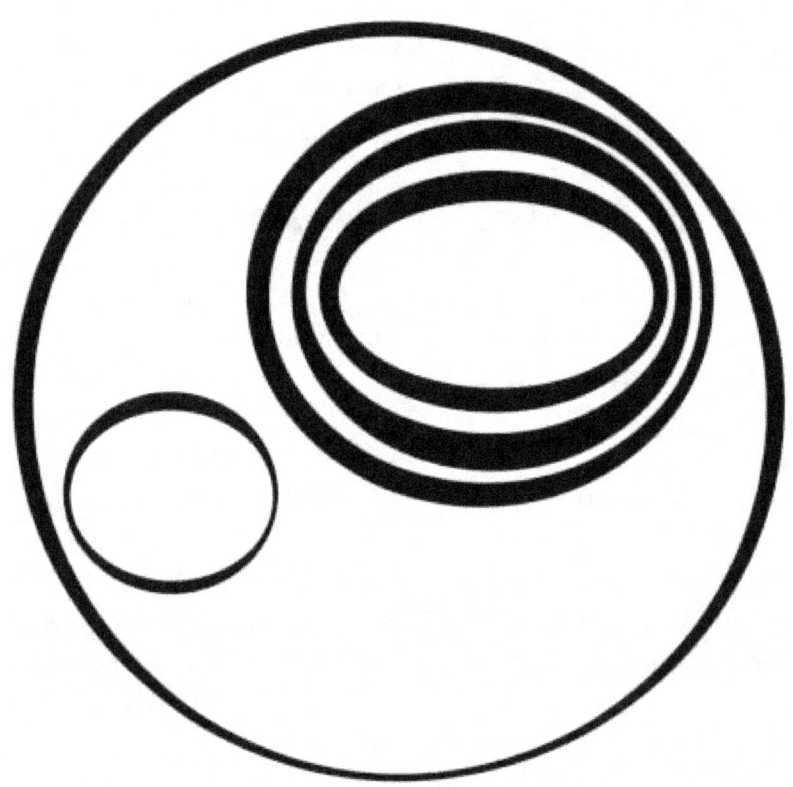

The Business Hero's Journey and Your Business Wonk

We've spent this entire workbook talking about your Business Hero's Journey. The journey taps into your emotions and the spiritual side of being a business owner. The other half of being an entrepreneur involves your wonk—your business know-how.

Though there are not any perfect relationships between the various stages of the journey and specific business knowledge that's needed, the journey can help you with your wonk, and your wonk can help you through the journey.

Let's talk wonk for a moment. A wonk is someone who has extensive knowledge about a subject. For lack of a better term, a nerd. So if you get your wonk on, then you are channeling your inner business nerd. It may not be a sexy image, or maybe it is. Because when you tap into your wonk you are putting your thoughts and desires into action.

If we think about many spiritual concepts such as the Law of Attraction, there is a mental/emotional component and an action/physical component. The wonk helps with the action/physical. A business owner can wish for more customers, but if she looks at some new marketing ideas there's a good chance she'll have greater success than from wishing alone. This doesn't mean that the spiritual concepts don't work. For many they do without any action. However, for the large majority of us we need to take physical action too. That's why we need our wonks.

We activate our wonk by asking one question:

What business information or action do I need right now?

That's it. We ask that question and we are not afraid of the answer. The last part is key. Do not be afraid of the answer your intuition (or your coach or best friend or mentor or whomever) tells you. It may be that you need to learn marketing or SEO or some other really in depth aspect of being a business owner. Maybe you need to redo your website or write a book! The action may be big and bold or small and subtle. Either way, it's your wonk speaking to you.

Learn to trust your wonk. Use those spiritual skills to know when something feels right and apply them to your business decisions. If you feel out of your depth when dealing with your wonk—with business concepts and ideas—don't panic. Remember that no one is born immediately knowing this and that you can learn. Anyone can learn.

Start to love the business concepts and ideas that power your work. It may be difficult. I know of very few people who love accounting or spreadsheets. Discovering new integrations or ways to make tech work for you may not excite you. It can.

Think about ways to add wonk to your woo and you'll find your journey to be a better one for you and for your business.

How to tap into your inner wonk?

- Find some aspect of your business, perhaps it's the technology, marketing, finances, or customer retention and research it. Make it your business to know as much about this as possible.
- Contemplate ways to integrate new strategies into your work. Remember, doing the same old thing and expecting different results is the definition of insanity.
- Track your cash flow. Really track it. Become best friends with your accounting program or your accountant.
- Look at what the brands you use in your daily life do. Why do you buy them? What draws you to their commercials?
- Conversely, think about the brands you hate. Why?

Where do you go from here?

Throughout the course of this workbook you've been given a lot of information. We've covered the five stages of the Business Hero's Journey. The circular and cyclical nature of the Business Hero's Journey has been covered. And finally, we've chatted a bit about your wonk. That's a lot of information.

The next obvious question is: **where do you go from here?**

I have a lot of great resources and they're listed at the end of this workbook. But this isn't about me and the tools I have that can help you; it's about you! Your business, your wonk, and your woo…how to integrate them and what to do with them.

1) Now that you've gone through the workbook take some time to think about your journey. What stage are you in right now? Return to that section and really dig deep.
2) Don't forget to invite your wonk to play. What business knowledge or process do you need right now?
3) Begin to shape your journey. Think about what *Freedom* and *Mastery* look like to you and how you can achieve it. What step can you take right now?
4) Honor your feelings and take the time you need.
5) Get help. Reach out.

Your next action is one step. That's where you go from here. Just one thing, one step, one action that you can do to move forward. It is easy to get overwhelmed by the entire process, especially if you are at the beginning of your journey. Take a deep breath and look for one step. One thing that you can do.

And remember, I'm right here beside you.

Begin your Better Business Journey

Introduction To The Business Hero's Journey: 7 Weeks To Get On Course and Stay There

Week 1: Introduction To The Business Hero's Journey: During our first week you'll learn exactly what a hero's journey is, the primary reason why you're stuck and how to shift into the next stage.

Week 2: The Call To Adventure: In this week, learn the power of the call, how to embrace your sacred entrepreneur self, and why it's important that you refuse the call.

Week 3: Road of Trials: It isn't easy being an entrepreneur so learn why it's important you travel the road of trials, what to do when you wind up overwhelmed and fighting it, and when you should allow yourself to be tempted.

Week 4: Triumph: Embrace the rejuvenating power of a breakthrough, and celebrate your triumphs. Bathe in the moment of bliss. Explore why these steps occur when they do and how they can transform not just you, but also your business.

Week 5: The Return Road: Discover the ideal time in an entrepreneur's journey to take the return road and why it doesn't mean failure. This is the most important crossroads of the Business Hero's Journey; the lessons of this week will make you rethink everything (in a good way).

Week 6: Mastery: Embrace the power of your mastery and learn what true freedom means.

Week 7: Moving Forward On Your Journey: In our final week we'll talk about embracing the journey, even when the universe appears to be fighting you, and how to choose the steps you're on to power your business to new heights.

Please join me in "Introduction To The Business Hero's Journey: 7 Weeks To Get On Course and Stay There"

Enroll by visiting http://www.businessstoryacademy.com and visit the store. Choose classes.

Put the Entrepreneur Priestess on Your Team

As a spiritual entrepreneur, there's a good chance you got woo. You have a lot of woo, mojo, positive vibes, and powerful gifts. You may not have wonk. Or you may not think you're capable of real wonkitude. (That's like attitude, but with powerful wonk behind it.)

You don't have to find your wonk alone. Put the Entrepreneur Priestess on your team.

I don't want you to walk through your Business Hero's Journey alone. Let me walk beside you, be your guide, your mentor, even your mojo maker.

- ❖ Discover clarity so you know exactly what your next business step should be.
- ❖ Get focused and get it done.
- ❖ Dive into business concepts without fear and with the knowledge that you can do this.
- ❖ Embrace the moment without fear or judgment so you can listen to your intuition
- ❖ Come up with solid, actionable plans so you never have to struggle with overwhelm or uncertainty.

Contact me to schedule your free Business Story Strategy Session and let's talk!
http://businessstoryacademy.com/about/contact-me/

Don't forget:

This workbook is taken from the class *Weekend Journey: Explore the Business Hero's Journey*. The entire class contains this workbook and a two hour audio. You may purchase the CD on Amazon.com or, you may upgrade to the entire class by visiting my website.

You can also download the free PDF of this book at the same page.

WEB ADDRESS:
http://businessstoryacademy.com/xtras/wj_ebhj_special/
   Use the password "printspecial"

www.ingramcontent.com/pod-product-compliance
Lightning Source LLC
Chambersburg PA
CBHW081903170526
45167CB00007B/3127